NO COMPROMISE

Rune Larsen

No Compromise

Published by Author - Rune Larsen

www.SecretRevelations.com

ISBN; 978-82-93411-23-9

Cover design by Panagiotis Lampridis

Preface

The right way or the wrong way

You drive a car, and suddenly it starts to rain. Your clean and pretty windshield is now suddenly covered by water and dirt. Immediately, your excellent visibility became replaced with zero visibility. There is a crisis, and something needs to be done. You can't stop either, because right behind you there are a 100.000 lbs heavy truck. You must continue. But if you do not do anything for the next 2 seconds, it's not just you and your passengers who are at risk, but you are also a danger to all on-coming traffic and your surroundings.

Then there is only one thing to do, grab the lever that is on the right side of the steering wheel, pull it down, and then the wind-shield wipers start to work.
The wipers begin to clean, and water, flies, dirt, and other legumes become washed away.
-You have a tool that is customized for you to see.

The same is for a Christian. He has tools from the Lord to use regarding preaching the gospel to a lost and dying world.
-But if you do not want to use the tools, which the primary key to release is obedience, you will be blinded by your disobedience.

Listen;

"In whom, the god of this world hath **blinded the minds** of them which **believe not**, lest the light of the glorious gospel of

Christ, who is the image of God, should shine unto them.''
(2 Corinthians 4:4 KJV)

(1) Blinded
Blinded is from the Greek word, Tuphloo, and it means; To make blind, to obscure.
-Your unbelief makes you blind, so you cannot see the truth. (Discern-understand)

(2) Minds
In the same verse, we also read the word: **minds**. Minds are from the Greek word; Noema, and it means; A perception, i.e., Purpose, or (by implication) the intellect, mind, thought.

In this verse, we see that Satan has full access to your intellect and your thoughts. When Satan can blind your thoughts, your thoughts are spiritual. In the same way, your words are spiritual. Everything you say, everything you think is spiritual.
-Therefore, everything we do and think must be done according to God's revealed word, not according to our latest seductive thoughts and temptations.

(3) Believe not
Let us take a look at; Believe not. Greek; Apistos. Apistos has several meanings; One of them is; **Infidel**. Infidel means; Those who do not believe the central principles of one's faith. (literally cheating on their faith)

If we choose to participate in what the Bible refers to as sin, we

are immediately one who promotes Satan's kingdom. Not only are we seduced, but we have chosen to be so.
We cannot blame Satan for this because we are responsible for all our actions ourselves.

When you decide to be obedient to the Lord, you will begin to see and understand. This is not a one-time 'event,' but something you have to live in daily.

The first step of obedience is;
Seek God with all your heart, start by witnessing to others what God has done for you.

Listen;
"For you were once darkness, but now you are light in the Lord. **Walk as children of light**." (Ephesians 5:8)

But what happens when you disobey the Lord? Well, then you are an infidel, and Satan is free to take over your steering wheel.

The window cleaners that had made your vision and understanding clear will now be reversed.
-The god of this world has blinded the unbelieving minds.

The reversal of the wipers means that you now no longer see clearly, nor understand what is very necessary for you to understand.
Humility always goes hand in hand with obedience. And if the Lord says something, you must be willing to do so.
If not - a life like a blinded disbeliever. (Disobedient)

Listen;

"He who says, "I know Him," and does not keep His commandments, **is a liar**, and the truth is not in him. But whoever keeps His word, truly the love of God is perfected in him. By this we know that we are in Him." (1 John 2:4-5)

Notes;

_____

_____

_____

_____

_____

_____

_____

_____

Intro

No Compromise is a Bible-based discipleship workbook, and it uses the Holy Bible as the textbook.

It contains 13 lessons, with approx. 8-18 questions each lesson. This gives you a total of more than 150 questions for you to work with.

The purpose of a workbook like this is that you should work with the Bible yourself to understand the questions. Do not look straight into the answer, but even ponder the question itself. If there is a Bible verse in a question, look up the scripture, and work on it.

Some questions will manifest themselves when reading the Bible verse, while others will require more of you, depending on your spiritual understanding.

Getting into the revealed Word of God is a demanding process that can only be entered through obedience to God's Word.

The more you show the Lord willingness to be a disciple for Him, the more understanding of the Lord and His words you will have.

Some of the questions seem simple. But starting to work purposefully with scripture is necessary to engage the doer of the word in you. (James 1:22)

Your biblical foundations and actions make way for wisdom and understanding. (Revelations)

The Bible

The Bible is not a book for man only to read, nor is it an entertaining book. It is a divine book from the Lord Himself, and it contains lots of stories that are meant to give us further revelations.

The Bible is a workbook and should be worked with as you go to work daily.

Let us look at the following example from chapter one in this book;

1. What will happen if you do not forgive others their trespasses? (Matthew 6:14)

_____

_____

Answer; The Lord will not forgive your trespasses.

Here you see question 1 and the answer you see below the drawn line.

The questions you will encounter from Chapter 1 will not have the answers shown like here. They are in a separate chapter after chapter 1-2-3 etc.

Do not look them up in advance, but work with the questions through the Bible to find the revelations in them.

2. Without Divine Revelations, people will perish.

What does revelation mean? It means to uncover something that has been hidden.
Revelations cannot be understood with the reasoning of the mind. -They are revealed to you by the Lord.

(1) What does the bible say about revelations?

Let us read the first part in 1 Peter 4:11; "If any man speak, let him speak **as** the **oracles** of God…"

If any man speaks, now we need to pay attention to what we shall do here.
The next word is **oracles**. Oracles are from the Greek word; Logion, and it means; An **utterance** (Revelation of God) - oracle.
-Utterance; A spoken word. (From God to you)

Then the practical use of 1 Peter 4:11 is like this; He that speaks (whosoever) he shall speak from his divine revelations.
-Nothing else.

Scriptures; Not for quoting purposes, but for teaching purposes

Under no circumstances, you shall quote scriptures to the left and right like many are doing today. If someone is doing it, the question is not how spiritual matured they are, but it shows that they are not at all mature in Christ.
-Under no circumstances, you shall speak-teach-preach anything that is not revealed from God and to you.

(2) What will happen if you do not have any revelations in your Christian life?

-And pay attention to what is written here. The word of God is what matters, never your feelings or what your 'kind' pastor says. (If you have one)

Listen;
"Where there is no **vision**, the people **perish**: but he that keepeth the law, happy is he." (Proverbs 29:18 KJV)

We read the word **vision**. It is from the Hebrew word; Chazown. It means; **Revelations**.

The next word in Proverbs 29:18 is; **Perish**; Hebrew: para, and it means; **Spiritual death - backslide**.

Those who not obtain revelations from the Lord will backslide into spiritual death!

Backslide into spiritual death? Now you understand how serious you must take the Lord in your life.

James 1:22
Let's have a look at what the book of James says about how you shall relate to God's word; **Faith without action is dead**.

"But be doers of the word, and not hearers only, deceiving yourselves." (James 1:22)

CONTENTS

Basic Bible Teaching

1. What will happen if you do not forgive others their trespasses? (Matthew 6:14)

_____

_____

2. How big faith do you need to pray for the sick? (Luke 17:6)

_____

_____

3. What will happen to the wicked? (1 Corinthians 6:9)

_____

_____

2

4. What kind of love does God offer in John 3:16?
(2 Peter 3:9)

_____

_____

_____

5. If you have a relationship with the Lord, what will you do? (John 14:15)

_____

_____

6. What is the current status of planet earth?
(1 John 5:19)

_____

_____

7. What will happen with a slanderer if he does not repent? (Psalm 101:5)

_____

_____

8. What do our words reveal? (Matthew 12:33-35)

_____

_____

9. What will happen to all the liars? (Proverbs 19:9)

_____

10. What lies in the Gospel? (Romans 1:17)

_____

_____

11. What are the names of the 12 Apostles?
(Matthew 10:2-4)

_____

_____

_____

_____

_____

12. Who replaced Judas Iscariot? (Acts 1:23-26)

_____

13. What did Jesus refer to every time Satan tempted him? (Matthew 4:4, 7, 10)

4:4 _____

4:7 _____

4:10 _____

14. Is repentance enough to be saved? Or do we need to repent and be born again? (John 3:3)

1 _____

2 _____

_____

_____

15. For what purpose did Jesus come into the world? (1 John 3:8)

_____

_____

16. What must all believers do? (Hebrews 12:14)

_____

17. What will happen if you do not pursue Holiness? (Hebrews 12:14)

_____

18. Will God save the wicked? (John 3:5)

_____

_____

Notes;

_____

_____

_____

_____

Answers to Lesson 1
Basic Bible Teaching

1. The Lord will not forgive your trespasses.

Love and forgiveness are the most powerful words and actions humanity can act on.

2. Just believe, and then act on what you believe. (Mark 16:18)

3. They will not inherit God's kingdom.

4. God's love offers an open door for the wicked to enter for repentance for their sins, become born again, live a life with Christ in obedience in this world.

5. You will keep His commandments.

6. The whole world lies in the power of the evil (Satan) one.

7. The punishment of God will hit slander.

8. Our words reveal what's in our hearts.

9. They will perish.

10. In the Gospel lies the truthfulness of God.

11.

Now the names of the twelve apostles are these: first, Simon, who is called **Peter**, and **Andrew** his brother; **James** the son of Zebedee, and **John**, his brother; **Philip** and **Bartholomew**; **Thomas** and **Matthew** the tax collector; **James** the son of Al-phaeus, and **Lebbaeus**, whose surname was Thaddaeus; **Simon** the Cananite, and **Judas Iscariot**, who also betrayed Him.

12. Matthias.

13. It is written.

Jesus referred only to what the scripture says. His fleshly opinions was not an option. The same is for you today.
-What is written, is what we act on. (James 1:22)

14.
(1) No.

(2) We must repent and turn our lives to Christ Jesus and be born again. This is the first step in a life with Christ.

15. To destroy the works of Satan.

16. Pursue Holiness.

Step number 1 into the path of Holiness after you have been born again; Start to witness to those around you what Jesus Christ has done for you. Then you will grow into Mark 16:15.

17. You will not see the Lord.

18. Only if they repent, turn to Christ, and become born again.

Notes;

_____

_____

_____

_____

_____

_____

_____

_____

Self-denial

A Definition of Humility (humbleness)

The world defines humility as a lowering of oneself in relation to others. A state of being humble, freedom of pride, and arrogance. Having a modest opinion or estimate of one's worth.

-To be a doormat for others have nothing to do with humility.

Humbleness is power under control.

The opposite of humbleness is pride

Lets read James 4:6; "God <u>resists</u> the proud, but gives grace to the humble."

The word **resists**. Greek; Antitiasso, which means; To range in battle against.

-When the Lord is in a battle against the proud, it is because proud people are doing the same against Him with their pride and disbelief.

Matthew 18:1-4 says;

"At that time the disciples came to Jesus, saying, "Who then is greatest in the kingdom of heaven?"

Then Jesus called a little child to Him, set him in the midst of them, and said, "Assuredly, I say to you, unless you are converted and become as little children, you will by no means enter the kingdom of heaven. Therefore whoever humbles himself as this little child is the greatest in the kingdom of heaven."

Take note;
It does not say, Be childish. Then we become like doormats for others. (Remember higher in this section?)
-It says, Whoever humbles himself as this little child is the greatest in the kingdom of heaven.
He is not saying that we are to be childish but childlike. That is a huge difference.

Children are naturally humble. And whoever is humble, is teachable to Christ and life's realities.
-The Lord cannot fill a person with divine revelations who are already full of themselves.

1. **In Psalm 49:15, we read**, "But God will redeem my soul from the power of the grave, for He shall receive me. Selah."

What does this verse mean?

_____

_____

_____

_____

2. Let us read Matthew 16:24;

"Then Jesus said to His disciples, "If anyone desires to come after Me, let him <u>deny</u> himself, and take up his cross, and follow Me.""

Notes;
In this scripture, we read the word deny. Deny also means; To abstain; Restrain oneself from doing or enjoying something.

Abstain; Verb (used without object) to hold oneself back voluntarily, especially from something regarded as improper or unhealthy. To refrain deliberately and often with an effort of self-denial from an action or practice.

All the works of the flesh, all kinds of denial to be a doer of the word the way Christ tells us to do it, is nothing but a significant hindrance in all Christianity.
One thing is that you will never enter into the path of Holiness if you are not willing to abstain from all fleshly activities.

There can be written books about this subject, but it is much more vital that you start to obey Christ in all matters of life. If you chose Christ, you would begin to understand small things.

3. Self-deception is common to the wicked.

"He shall go to the generation of his fathers; They shall never see **light**. A man who is in honor yet does not understand, Is like the beasts that perish." (Psalm 49:19-20)

The word **light**, Hebrew: ra'ah, means visions.

It is not the 'pastor's' vision you shall take part in. It is not the 'congregation's' vision you shall take part in, cause in these 'visions' it tends to be nothing but control.

You are the one who must have the vision of obedience in Christ. It is you who must decide whether to follow Christ, as the scripture says.
If you have no visions about your obedience to Christ, nor being a servant for others, no vision about you preaching the gospel to the lost, it is because of self-deception.

4. Self-deception turns into thoughts like;

(1) Deuteronomy 29:19 _____

_____

(2) Proverbs 14:12 _____

_____

(3) Isaiah 56:12 _____

_____

(4) Luke 18:11 _____

_____

(5) Psalm 10:11_____

_____

(6) Psalm 10:6_____

_____

(7) Matthew 7:21_____

_____

(8) Revelation 3:17_____

_____

5. Examples on self-denial;

(1) James and John. (Mark 1:16-20)

(2) The first Christians. (Acts 2:45)

(3) Moses. (Hebrews 11:24-25)

(4) The poor widow. (Luke 21:4)

(5) Paul. (Acts 20:24)
(6) The Apostles. (Matthew 19:27)

6. Self-denial is practiced by;

(1) Galatians 5:24_____

_____

(2) 1 Peter 2:11_____

_____

(3) Romans 14:20-21_____

_____

(4) Luke 3:11_____

_____

(5) 1 Corinthians 10:23_____

_____

(6) 1 Peter 4:2_____

_____

(7) Titus 2:12 - Romans 6:12_____

_____

(8) Luke 14:33_____

_____

(9) Matthew 8:21-22_____

_____

(10) Matthew 10:38_____

_____

(11) Matthew 16:25-26_____

_____

(12) Romans 8:13_____

_____

(13) 2 Peter 1:4_____

_____

_____

_____

_____

7. Here you have some scriptures to meditate on regarding humility;

Ephesians 4:12, Philippians 2:3, Proverbs 11:2, 1 Peter 3:3-4, James 4:10, Colossians 3:12, Proverbs 29:23, James 3:13, Matthew 11:29-30, Proverbs 18:12, Mark 9:35, Proverbs 15:33.

8. The character of the New Man;

What does Colossians 3 say?

(1) Vers 1_____

_____

(2) Vers 2_____

_____

(3) Vers 8_____

_____

(4) Vers 12_____

_____

_____

(5) What is above these things? (Verse 14)

_____

_____

9. What happens to those who are not rooted in Christ? (Luke 8:13)

_____

_____

10. What will the believers inherit? (Hebrews 1:14)

_____

11. What shall you do with the words you are speaking? (Proverbs 13:3)

_____

_____

_____

_____

12. Let us read 1 John 5:2;

"By this, we know that we love the children of God when we love God and keep His commandments."

What is your love for God? (1 John 5:3)

_____

_____

_____

Those who do not tolerate the healthy doctrine, their no to the Lord, then become greater than His Yes.

Notes;

_____

_____

_____

_____

_____

_____

Answers to Lesson 2
Self-Denial

1. Death and Hades have seized on everyone who trusts in himself and what he has.

4. Self-deception turns into thoughts like;

(1) We can have peace in sin.

(2) Our own ways are right.

(3) We will live long.

(4) We are better than others.

(5) God does not see our sins.

(6) We are out of danger.

(7) Spiritual gifts and the like give right to heaven.

(8) We are rich in spirituality.

6. Self-denial is practiced by;

(1) Crucify the flesh.

(2) Stay away from carnal desires.

(3) Seeking the best of others.

(4) Share with others.

(5) Forsake the permissible.

(6) Deny human desires.

(7) Deny wickedness and worldliness.

(8) Forsake everything.

(9) Sacrifice everything for Christ's sake.

(10) Take the cross up to follow Christ.

(11) The danger of neglecting.

(12) Salaried.

(13) Blessed result of.

8. The character of the New Man.

What does Colossians 3 say?

(1) Not carnality but Christ.

(2) Set (obedience) your mind on things above, not on things on the earth.

(3) **Put off** all these: anger, wrath, malice, blasphemy, filthy language out of your mouth.

(4) Live the new life, **put on** tender mercies, kindness, humility, meekness, longsuffering.

(5) Love.

9. Those who do not have roots fall away during the trials.

10. Salvation.

11. Guard our words. Distance yourself from all corrupt communications.

12. The love of God is that we keep His commandments. (Remember Mark 16:5?)

Notes;

_____

_____

_____

_____

_____

22

Notes;

Consequences

Most believers go through their lives without thinking much about their responsibilities to the Lord.
-A reluctance to be a doer of the word brings out blindness in their lives. (Remember the foreword in this book?)

When we see God's wrath through the Old Testament, it is because the people would not humble themselves before Him. Had they done so, the whole world situation today would have been different.
Believers today are nothing more humble than they were before. Therefore, we see spiritual confusion among those who claim to be Christians.
The consequence of not obeying the Lord will arouse His wrath today since He has not changed anything since the dawn of time. (Hebrews 13:8)

1. What are we doing if we say we do not have any sin? (1 John 1:10)

_____

_____

2. What are the wages of sin? (Romans 6:23)

_____

3. Will those who are not born again be saved? (John 3:3)

_____

4. What is the consequence of Adam's sin?
(Romans 5:12)

_____

_____

5. Is there anybody that has not sinned in this world?
(Romans 3:10)

_____

6. What is the consequence for those who practice homosexuality? (1 Corinthians 6:9-10)

_____

_____

_____

7. What is the consequence of not being a doer of the word, but a hearer only? (James 1:22)

8. Is there a consequence of using your pride to say no to the Lord's ways with your actions? (Proverbs 11:2)

9. What goes before destruction? (James 4:6)

10. Is there any consequence of going to a 'church' every Sunday, but have not been born again and living a life in the Lord's will? (John 3:3)

11. Are there consequences of not getting into the revelation knowledge?

_____

_____

12. What is the consequence of a self-righteous man?
(Proverbs 14:12)

_____

_____

13. Are God's commandments burdensome for you?
(1 John 5:3)

_____

14. Will God ever tempt you? (James 1:13)

_____

15. What is the consequence of not being born again?
(John 3:3)

_____

_____

_____

Answers to Lesson 3
Consequences

1. We make him (God) a liar.

"If we say that we have not sinned, we make Him a liar, and His word is not in us." (1 John 1:10)

Sin is trespassing into areas that are not allowed. If you do the opposite (your no to His yes) of what the Lord says, you are trespassing.

2. Death.

Wages of sin is death. Death means eternal damnation.
Eternal damnation is the result for all those who are living a life in the flesh.

In John 3:5, we read, "Jesus answered, "Most assuredly, I say to you unless one is born of water and the Spirit, he cannot enter the kingdom of God."

(1) Born of water means; This is our physical birth. Nine months you have been formed inside water in your mother's womb, and then she gave birth to you.

(2) Born of Spirit means; This is our Spiritual rebirth.
John 3:3 shows us the great importance of Spiritual rebirth;
"Most assuredly, I say to you, unless one is born again, he cannot see the kingdom of God."

3. No.

4. Sin and death came into the world.

5. No.

6. Yes. They will not inherit the kingdom of God.

7. You are deceiving yourself.

Lets read James 1:22. "But be doers of the word, and not hearers only, deceiving yourselves."

At the end of this verse, you find; Deceiving yourselves. The word: deceiving means; (1) Misreckon. (2) Beguile.

(1) **Misreckon**
-When you misreckon the word of God, you have believed a lie from Satan. Unwillingly you did not start acting on what God's word told you to but chose the lie instead.

For example, Christ gives all believers a mission commandment in Mark 16:15. This applies to you who read it.
If you did not believe this, you would misreckon the truth by believing the lie from Satan. And the lie is, I do not have 'that' call, or; My call is something else and so on.

(2) **Beguile**
The meaning of; beguile (a verb); To persuade, attract, or interest someone, sometimes to deceive them.

-Her beauty utterly beguiled him.

-The salesman beguiled him into buying a car he didn't want.

-Satan and all the disobedient 'believers' beguiles you with lies so that you do not see or start acting on the truth from the Lord.

Synonyms to beguile - Captivate, bewitch, spellbind.

When you listen to people that proclaim they do not have the call to preach the gospel to the lost, you are listening to captivating words.

Spoken captivating words from others - Deceiving thoughts from Satan. When you believe this like the example about the mission commandment in Mark 16:15, you have deceived yourself.

Even if you 'only' listened to the lies from others, you are the one who is responsible for making all the right desitions in your life.

-This is how you deceive yourself.

---

8. Yes.

Let's read Proverbs 11:2. "When pride comes, then comes shame. But with the humble is wisdom."

The word **pride** is from the Hebrew word zadown. It means; Arrogance, presumptuously, pride, proud.

The next word in Proverbs 11:2 is perhaps one of the most important words when it comes to pride and what will happen when we let pride into our lives and decisions.
-We read the word; **Shame**.
Shame is from the Hebrew word qalown. It means; dishonor, shame, **confusion**.

Let us reread Proverbs 11:2, but this time with a revelation; When you use pride in your life - actions, confusion will follow right away.
Here is one of the leading causes why believers do not want to preach the gospel to the lost. Many let pride controls their emotional decisions, listening to others and Satans deceiving thoughts instead of God's word. When you adapt confusion to your life as a believer, it will be hard to enter into an understanding (revelations) of who the Lord is and what He wants.
(For you)

_____

_____

9. Pride.

10. Yes. That person is not saved.

11. Yes. If you are not able to receive revelations from God's word, it is the revelation of the senses (Satans deceit) you have put your trust in.

Let's read Proverbs 29:18 from the King James Version of the Bible; "Where there is no vision, the people perish: but he that keepeth the law, happy is he."

(1) The word vision is from the Hebrew word: Chazown, and it means Revelation.

Here is a revelation to the word vision in Proverbs 29:18 with an explanation.
-If you do not have any revelations, you will be naked in your understanding of God's word and your ways with the Lord. If believers are naked in their faith, the armor of God is not on, and they are not of any use in the Lord's ministry. To put on the armor that Ephesians 6:13-17 shows us, you cannot pray and ask God to receive. You must start to walk with the Lord, and then your understanding will grow.

(2) The meaning of the word perish;
Perish, Hebrew; para. It means; Go back (backslide), naked.

Those who not obtain revelations from the Lord will backslide into spiritual death.
You glide straight back into the realm of unbelief and confusion. The place where Satan works intensely with you and those around you as an angel of light and pretends to be God.
-A naked believer is no match for Satan to conquer.

12. The end of his road is death.

Death. Do you remember question 2?

13. No.

If they are, you must ask your self what direction you are heading.

Attn;
We do not understand all the things written in the Bible at one time. Therefore there is of great importance that you are willing to follow the Lord the way He says.

Do you see the importance of being willing and not unwilling to be a doer of God's word?

Your answer;_____

14. No.

15. He, who is not born again is not saved.

Notes;

_____

_____

_____

_____

34

Notes;

_____

_____

_____

_____

_____

_____

_____

_____

_____

_____

_____

_____

_____

The marching order

1. Where do we stand after we have received salvation?

Listen;
"I am a <u>debtor</u> both to Greeks and to barbarians, both to wise and to unwise." (Romans 1:14)

For I am in debt;
The Christian has been rid of his guilty sin by repentance and faith in Christ, but at the very moment he gets rid of it, he comes into a new debt situation.
-Now it is the responsibility to bring the gospel to the world. (Mark 16:15)

2. The Lord has issued a commandment for you what to do for him. When you read this, either you discard it with your misunderstanding of the commandment, or you just love to live a life in the middle of the highway of self adored pride.

Let's have a look if you are a willing, obedient believer or not;

To all believers

The Lord has commissioned a marching order to all believers
that are born again. A marching order is an order to put themselves in motion to accomplish a task.

The marching order is not complicated if you are willing to obey
the Lord, but if you do not want, or have a different view on the
matter, it will be trouble.

Listen to what the Bible says;

The last Jesus said to His disciples was the mission commandment in Mark 16:15.

And He said to them, "Go into all the world and preach the
gospel to every creature. He who <u>believes</u> and is baptized will
be saved, but he who does not believe will be condemned."
(Mark 16:15-16)

Did Jesus command the disciples to go out in the whole world
and baptize people? No.
-Let's have a look with the eyes of revelation what Jesus says in
this scripture;

(1) It is not the unsaved Jesus is talking to: it is His disciples.

(2) And He said to them; Go into all the world and preach the
gospel to every creature.

(3) Pay attention to what happens next in verse 16; He who believes and is baptized will be saved, but he who does not believe
will be condemned.

He who believes?
Who shall believe and be baptized? It is the disciples Jesus is
talking to. The disciples must **believe the mission commandment** to go out in the whole world and preaching the gospel. If
they believe this and do what their faith proclaims, then they
must be baptized.

If you do not believe the mission commandment, what is the
point of being baptized when baptism is external evidence of
your faith?
If you don't believe the mission commandment, you are an unbeliever. The word unbeliever does not mean anything but disobedient.

What is faith?
Faith in the New Testament is understood as the **yes** of man to
the words and revelations of God, and therefore it will determine
the human relationship of God.
-Faith denotes a trusting devotion to God, as He is revealed in
Jesus Christ.

(4) What happens if the disciples (you) will not believe-obey
what Jesus is commanding in Mark 16:15? The last part of verse
16 gives us the answer, but he who does not believe (the mission
commandment) will be condemned.

38

"Fear God and keep His commandments, for this is man's all."
(Ecclesiastes 12:13)

3. What does the Lord say to all believers in Mark 16:15?

_____

_____

4. How should people come to faith through you?
(Romans 10:17)

_____

_____

5. The proclaimed Gospel is God's cure for sin.

Romans 10:17; Then comes the faith of the preaching one hearing, and the preaching of the words of Christ.

The word of Christ is the revealed word of God
The revealed word of God is the word that becomes alive and understandable. When you proclaim the revealed word, people will feel it touches them. People will know that here they must make a decision. People know in their spirit, in their interior that this is right, this is the truth.

"For I am not ashamed of the gospel of Christ, for it is the power of God to salvation for everyone who believes, for the Jew first and also for the Greek." (Romans 1:16)

How do you relate to what is written in Romans 1:16?
Are you ashamed of the command of Christ to preach the gospel to the lost, according to Mark 16:15?
-Are you ashamed of standing in front of someone who is on the way to eternal damnation in hell, preaching the life rescuing gospel of Jesus Christ to him?

Your answer;_____

_____

_____

6. To hear is to do.

This means something more than passively listening to what someone says.

When the Lord gives us a command, our work is to do. To hear is to do. James 1:22.
-If you only listen, you are trapped in the trap of unwillingness.

How do you activate what you hear?
Only when you adjust to what is said, one has heard with the heart, not only with the ears.

40

7. Who is your role model for your ministry? (John 13:15-17)

_____

8. Is there a consequence not to involve yourself in the mission commandment? (Mark 16:15)

_____

_____

_____

9.

Go Jesus say
All you say
I love it my way

If he is your Lord
you will run after
those who do not
understand God's accord

Blind shall see
sick will be healed
do you even care
about those who are hammered down
by Satans steel?

10. In Matthew 9:12, we read the word evil. Who shall continue to preach the gospel to the evil people in this world?

_____

11. What does Christ need? (Luke 10:2)

_____

_____

Notes;

_____

_____

_____

_____

_____

_____

_____

42

Answers to Lesson 4
The marching order

3. Go out in the whole world and preach the gospel to the lost.

4. Faith comes from preaching; You must preach the gospel to them.

How can people come to believe when you do not want to preach the gospel to them?

7. Jesus Christ.

8. Yes.

Ref; Question 2.4 in this chapter.

10. All who are born again. (Mark 16:15)

11. Christ needs workers, not sympathizers!

Whether you believe that the Lord has given you a mission command as described in Mark 16:15, or you don't.
-If you don't believe it, it is not faith you have, but unbelief.

A lukewarm 'believer' is standing on a landmine

Are you lukewarm? Or are you on fire for Jesus?

Your answer;_____

Notes;

Your obedience will show the fruits of good works. But if you are lukewarm, your relationship with God will not be as intended. Neither will you have a relationship with your neighbor who is characterized by obedience to the mission commandment of Christ.

Lukewarm means;

Cold in the spiritual sense. This is the man who, in his interior, is untouched by the influence of the word of God and the Spirit. Cold can also portray the one who, after losing his life in God, has fallen back to the level of the human being and the way of life.

Warm means;

Warm is the human being considered to have wholeheartedly dedicated his person with spirit, soul, and body to God.

Unlike the spiritual cold, the spiritual lukewarm once experienced the awakening and life-giving influence of God's Word and Spirit. But he does not pursue perfection, Philippians 3:12, or his moral course, 2 Peter 3:14, but lives in a false satisfaction with himself and his state, Revelation 3:17, in a false self-assessment, in self-deception, and lack addiction in the relationship with God, Revelation 3:20.

The lukewarm will not deny Christ, but in his self-righteousness, he closes out of the community with Christ. (Revelation 3:16)

1. There is one question from the Lord that must be answered for all those who are lukewarm. This question is not passed in this life or on the way into the heavenly life.

What is your answer to the vital question in Luke 6:46?

_____

_____

_____

_____

2. What will happen with a 'believer' that is lukewarm? (Revelation 3:16)

_____

3. How does James 4:17 relate to Mark 16:15?

4. **Listen;**

"For the time will come when they will not endure sound doctrine, but according to their own desires, because they have itching ears, they will heap up for themselves teachers; and they will turn their ears away from the truth, and be turned aside to fables." (2 Timothy 4:3-4)

Notes;

This is the state of most of the 'churches' today. Always go in and listen. But Jesus said; Go out in the whole world and preach the gospel.

5. Do you dear to take a look in the mirror? Do you dear to look Jesus in the eyes and tell him you are faithful to his mission commandment? (2 Corinthians 13:5)

6. Pride;

Let us summarize in simple terms what real pride is and how it works; A feeling of deep pleasure or satisfaction derived from one's achievements.

Countless 'believers' I have met on the streets in recent years. The strange thing is that most of them think they are where they should be with the Lord. But when you discern spiritually, it does not matter what they say with their mouths.
With the most substantial confidence, they are not susceptible to revelations in the form of a word or prophetic prosecution for the guidance. They are where they should be and are very happy with it.
-If I try to give them something, the attack comes in the form of; Don't tell me differently.

7. Are you obedient to the Lord, or comforted by this world? (1 John 2:15)

_____

8. What does Ephesians 4:1 tell you regarding the mission commandment?

_____

_____

9. What is written in John 14:21?

10. Are you one of those Jesus is talking about in Matthew 7:21?

Notes;

Answers to Lesson 5
A lukewarm 'believer' is standing on a landmine

1. ?

"But why do you call Me 'Lord, Lord,' and not do the things which I say?" (Luke 6:46)

The question here is not how much you believe or love the Lord: it is only a matter of obedience. If all believers had not received a mission commandment from the Lord, it would not have been necessary to use words like; Why do you call me Lord, Lord, and don't do what I say? (Commandeth)

2. He will be spat out.

A further answer is in chapter 4 question 2.4 - Are you on the winning team or in the hammock team?

"Every tree (that's you) that does not bear good fruit (to other people) is cut down and thrown into the fire." (Matthew 7:19)

A lukewarm will not open the door and let him who is Lord over all things inside.
There is one thing that needs to be mentioned about the Lord, and that is; When you open your door for him, you will be put to work immediately.

"Then He said to them all, "If anyone desires to come after Me, let him deny himself, and take up his cross daily, and follow Me." (Luke 9:23)

-This is your daily work as a witness for those around you on your path.

3. "Therefore, to him who knows to do good and does not do it, to him it is sin." (James 4:17)

Now you know the truth about Mark 16:15. Now you see one of the consequences.

5. ?

"Examine yourselves as to whether you are in the faith. (As a doer of the word)
Test yourselves. Do you not know yourselves, that Jesus Christ is in you? - unless indeed you are disqualified."
(2 Corinthians 13:5)

If your answer is yes; Then continue to obey. You can only grow from this point.

If your answer is no; Then you must ask yourself what direction you are heading.

"Because you say, 'I am rich, have become wealthy, and have need of nothing' - and do not know that you are wretched, miserable, poor, blind, and naked." (Revelation 3:17)

7. ?

Lordship is not to follow after others, or only to listen to what the word of God says, it is to walk with the Lord personally and be lead by the Holy Ghost. (Which will only happen to those who are willing to be a doer of the word)

"Do not love the world or the things in the world. If anyone loves the world, the love of the Father is not in him."
(1 John 2:15)

8. ?

"I, therefore, the prisoner of the Lord, beseech you to walk (in Mark 16:15) worthy of the calling with which you were called.."
(Ephesians 4:1)

9. "He who has My commandments (Mark 16:15) and keeps them, it is he who loves Me. And he who loves Me will be loved by My Father, and I will love him and manifest Myself to him."
(John 14:21)

10. "Not everyone who says to Me, 'Lord, Lord,' shall enter the kingdom of heaven, but he who does the will of My Father in heaven." (Matthew 7:21)
Notes;
The will of the Lord is that no one will end up in damnation, but come to the knowledge of truth and become saved. That's the only reason why God the Father sent His only begotten Son to the earth and be crucified on Calvary as the savior of the world.

God himself gave his life on Calvary, passed on the work to preach the Gospel of salvation to his disciples. Today believers respond to this great word from the Lord himself by turning their back to him and say, no, I am not called to be a witness or preach the Gospel to the lost.

Notes;

_____

_____

_____

_____

_____

_____

_____

_____

_____

52

Notes;

_____

_____

_____

_____

_____

_____

_____

_____

_____

_____

_____

_____

_____

Obedience brings forth holiness
Part 1

Without sanctification, no one will see the Lord

It is a word of truth, many knows, but few think about it. Most of the time, when we read this passage, we pass it as nothing happened.

You are incorporated into sanctification the day you are saved. Still, if you shall continue on the path of sanctification, it is only by obeying the written word of the Lord.

Sanctification is to be part of the mind of Christ and to live in accordance with this mind in daily succession to Christ.

1. What does Christ want in 1 Timothy 2:4?

_____

_____

2. How shall you act on question 1? (Mark 16:15)

_____

3. In the ministry of the saint, man is sanctified (Mark 16:15)

-Then you are characterized more and more of God's holy being.

The fruits of sanctification;

-A walk in the light; Ephesians 5:8.

-Goodness, humility, meekness, long-suffering, being able to endure others, forgiving minds; Colossians 3:12-13.

4. What does Hebrews 12:14 means?

_____

_____

5. The largest rescue operation in the universe

The Sinless Blood of Jesus Christ - The Blood Sent From God Yahweh in Heaven, Down to Earth, and into Christ.

-Christ's victory march towards Calvary, the reconciliation's victory over sin, a victory that was won for you and me.

He gave his life - No one could take it!

When Christ gave up His Spirit, His blood was sent back to heaven, sprinkled over the mercy seat that is the God of Yahweh's throne, was approved by the Lord as atonement for our sins.

After the blood was approved, Christ once again stood before the disciples. This time, He said; Look, touch me. The blood was left on Hillastarion. (Mercy seat)
Therefore, the scripture says; He stood there with flesh and bones.

6. What is the way of sanctification, and why does the Lord command you to walk in the path of holiness. (John 14:12)

_____

_____

_____

7. What is necessary to win people for Christ? (1 Peter 2:12)

_____

_____

8. What is it written in Luke 11:35?

_____

_____

9. What is the flesh, and what happens when we exercise carnal actions?

The action of the flesh is manifestations of the thoughts of Satan coming to our minds.
-Satan sends thoughts that you gladly accept by saying yes, thank you. Sin was born in your yes, then it gives birth to death in your action.
The power of the flesh draws us away from God's holiness in our lives. If we do not emphasize the fruits of the Spirit, it is our flesh that is our driving force throughout the day.

10. How does sanctification manifest in our lives, what is the first thing to look at without functioning in the distinction between the spirits?

_____

_____

_____

Notes;

_____

_____

_____

Answers to Lesson 6
Obedience brings forth holiness - Part 1

1. Christ wants all people to be saved and to come to a knowledge of the truth.

2. Go out in the whole world and preach the gospel.

4. None. It means all so-called believers and non-believers.

6. John 14:12 says; Most assuredly, I say to you, he (that's you) who believes in Me, the works that I do he will do also; and greater works than these he will do, because I go to My Father."

He who believes in Me, the works that I do he will also do. And what kind of work did Christ do? He was always on his way with His gospel to the lost. (Matthew 9:35)
-Like Christ, you shall do the same. (Mark 16:15)

We shall shine for those who live in the dark - We are the representative of Christ for them. It is the Lord they are to see in us.
-If you live a life in the flesh, it is the flesh and wickedness that will shine. Then the light has already been extinguished in you. If the light is off, you cannot win people for Christ either. It will then be a carnal affair and not a spiritual revelation and demonstration of God's Kingdom for the one who does not believe.

7. Holiness is necessary to be able to win people for Christ.

True sanctification manifests itself in its work to its neighbor.

8. See to it, then, that the light within you is not darkness.

This can only be done by keeping you in the path of the sanctification of obedience.

10. Like Christ - Always on the way to our neighbor.
(Mark 16:15)

Notes;

_____

_____

_____

_____

_____

_____

_____

_____

_____

Obedience brings forth holiness
Part 2

1. What has Sanctification to do with Matthew 22:39?

_____

_____

2. What does 2 Corinthians 6:14 mean for you?

_____

_____

_____

_____

3. What does the Bible tell you in 1 Peter 1:15-16?

_____

_____

4. What does God call you to do in;

(1) 1 Thessalonians 4:7_____

_____

_____

(2) Romans 12:1_____

_____

_____

5. **You shall live in holiness;**

The following scripture is a self-study regarding holiness.

Acts 26:18 - 1 Corinthians 6:11 - 2 Peter 3:11.

Your notes;

_____

_____

_____

_____

_____

6. What shall you present to God? (Romans 6:13. 19)

_____

_____

7. What is the believer created for after the new birth? (Ephesians 4:24)

_____

_____

8. What kind of attitude shall you have to Sanctification? (Hebrews 12:14 - 2 Peter 3:11)

_____

_____

9. What shall a servant of God be? (Titus 1:8)

_____

10. Mention some motives for Sanctification;

(1) John 15:8_____

_____

(2) Romans 12:1-2_____

_____

(3) 2 Peter 3:11_____

_____

(4) 1 Thessalonians 5:23_____

_____

11. What does the Lord say about the Sanctification in 1 Corinthians 6:9-11?

_____

_____

12. What does the Sanctification consist of?
(1 Thessalonians 5:22)

_____

_____

_____

13. Why is Sanctification necessary for our own Christian life? (Matthew 6:24 - Romans 6:16. 3)

_____

_____

14. In Mark 16:15, we see the Lord's commandment to all believers. Why is Sanctification important in this context? (1 Peter 2:12)

_____

_____

15. If the Lord says that there will be no prayer-answers without Sanctification and that no one can inherit the kingdom of God without, how shall we come into Sanctification when we read in Romans 6:19 that Sanctification comes only from obedience?

Then comes a question that you must answer before the Lord; If you do not want to go into the world with His gospel, and we see that obedience involves Sanctification, but you do not want to go, how are you going to get into the kingdom of God?

Your answer;_____

_____

_____

_____

16. The fruit of holiness; A walk in the light (Ephesians 5:8)

-Mercy, goodness, humility, meekness, long-suffering, being able to endure others, forgiving minds. (Colossians 3:12)

17. Not the visible, but the invisible

"While we do not look at the things which are seen, but at the things which are not seen. For the things which are seen are temporary, but the things which are not seen are eternal."
(2 Corinthians 4:18)

Notes;

_____

_____

_____

_____

_____

Answers to Lesson 7
Obedience brings forth holiness - Part 2

1. Love your neighbor brings this forth; True sanctification manifests itself in its work to its neighbor.

The holiness that reveals itself in the person and life of Jesus appears in the servant's figure. The whole of Jesus' life is in the ministry for his neighbor. He was always on his way to fellow human beings.

In the light of Jesus' life, we see that the great word of sanctification is ministering to his neighbor. (Matthew 20:26-27)
-See John 13:2-17 for more info.

-If you do not have a clear picture of who your neighbor is, it is all the people around you at any given time.

"Just as the Son of Man did not come to be served, but to serve, and to give his life as a ransom for many." (Matthew 20:28)

2. Do not be unequally yoked together with **unbelievers**. For what fellowship has righteousness with lawlessness? And what communion has light with darkness?

How shall those who live in the light have anything in common with the one who has stepped out of the light?
-We let the scripture interpret;

(1)

Unbelievers; Greek; Apistos; One who does not believe. Infidel.

Infidel is a derogatory term used when someone does not believe the central principles of one's religion.
-Unbelievers in this context mean in all simplicity; Disobedience to God.

'Believers' use their disbelief to justify themselves, through the scriptures above God and you.

(2) Light and darkness
When you are an obedient Christian, you are living in the light.
If you are a disobedient Christian, you are not living in the light.

What kind of communion can it be with the one who believes in the written word of God, and the one who does not believe, for example, Mark 16:15?
-None!

If you want to find out if a believer is disobedient, it will not be done with long interrogating questions.
-Here it must be distinguished spiritually, nothing else.

Homework;
Read Ephesians 4:17-32. The word **mind** in verse 23 means;
Thought-Feeling-Will-**Understanding**.

3. "But as He who called you is holy, **you also be holy in all your conduct**, because it is written, "Be holy, for I am holy." (1 Peter 1:15-16)

4.
(1) "For God did not call us to uncleanness, but in holiness." (1 Thessalonians 4:7)

(2)
"I beseech you therefore, brethren, by the mercies of God, that you present your bodies a living sacrifice, holy, acceptable to God, which is your reasonable service." (Romans 12:1)

6. Present your limbs as a tool for God. (Romans 6:13. 19)

7. The believers are after the new birth created for sanctification.

8. Must chase after sanctification.

9. Holy.

10.
(1) The glory of God.

(2) God's mercy.

(3) This world's perishability.

(4) The Day of Jesus Christ.

11. No one can inherit the kingdom of God without sanctification.

12. Keeping From All Evil - 1 Thessalonians 5:22.

The first word in this passage is the word abstain. Abstain means; Restrain oneself from doing or enjoying something. -Enjoy something? Suddenly it is you who are in the center and not Satan. It is your fleshly activities that you must be willing daily to let go of.

The next word we shall look at it in 1 Thessalonians 5:22 is evil. Evil also means the devil. If you're going to stay away from all Satan's evil schemes, you must exercise discernment throughout the day.
Without obedience to the written word of God, it will be impossible to enter into a full understanding of how Satan can fool you.

13. We cannot love God and the world at the same time.

14. So we can win people for God.

Notes;

_____

_____

_____

Obedience brings Revelations and Prayer answers

1. Abide in Jesus Christ.

Listen;
"Every branch in Me that does not bear fruit He takes away; and every branch that bears fruit He prunes, that it may bear more fruit." (John 15:2)

The same verse from the King James version;
"Every branch in me that beareth not fruit he taketh away: and every branch that beareth fruit, he **purgeth** it, that it may bring forth more fruit."

We read the word **purgeth**. It means; Removing impure things.

If you are obedient to God's word and commandments, you will be helped-learned-trained up-guided by the Lord to continue your growth. This is meant to you in singularity, not through a so-called 'church.'
-More info in John 14:26.

2. Obedience to the Lord is the only way to walk.

"**Abide** in me, and I in you. As the branch cannot bear fruit of itself, except it abide in the vine; no more can ye, except ye abide in me." (John 15:4 - King James Version)

The word abide means; Accept or act in accordance with a rule - decision. **Stand thine own**.
-Here we see how the Lord wants to train you up personally so that you can stand. If you lean on a 'fellowship,' you will never be able to stand thine own.

Definition of abiding;

(1) **To bear patiently**
-Yes, Lord. I will start obeying Mark 16:15 by reaching out to the lost, and I know that signs and wonder shall follow, cause you have said that you are with me, and also you said that you would never leave me or forsake me.

(2) **To accept without objection**
-Yes, Lord, I will abide in (accept) your mission commandment in Mark 16:15.

Synonyms to abide; Obey, follow, to accept.

Accept;
When you accept God's word, you are in a position to believe it. This is not trying to understand the word upfront.

(3) **Obey;**

If you say that Jesus is your Lord, but will not obey Him, He is not your Lord. (The word Lord means; He who decides)

-If He is your Lord, you will not have any issues to follow Him.

(4) **Follow;**

To follow; Is to do the same as Christ did to His lost sheep and to obey what He says through His word.

3. Why did Jesus come to earth? (Luke 19:10)

_____

_____

4. How shall people know the truth about the gospel?

_____

_____

5. Have you accepted that Jesus has given you a mission commandment? (Mark 16:15)

Your answer;_____

_____

_____

6. Are you acting on God's word in accordance with Mark 16:15?

Your answer;_____

_____

7. God will not hear the prayers of those who;

(1) **Despise God's call**
"Because I have called and you refused, I have stretched out my hand and no one regarded, because you disdained all my counsel, and would have none of my rebuke, I also will laugh at your calamity; I will mock when your terror comes, when your terror comes like a storm, and your destruction comes like a whirlwind, when distress and anguish come upon you. "Then they will call on me, but I will not answer; They will seek me diligently, but they will not find me." (Proverbs 1:24-28)

(2) **Is doubting**
"But let him ask in faith, with no doubting, for he who doubts is like a wave of the sea driven and tossed by the wind."
(James 1:6)

(3) **Is self-righteous**
"The Pharisee stood and prayed thus with himself, 'God, I thank You that I am not like other men-extortioners, unjust, adulterers, or even as this tax collector." (Luke 18:11)

"Woe to you, scribes and Pharisees, hypocrites! For you devour widows' houses, and for a pretence make long prayers. Therefore you will receive greater condemnation." (Matthew 23:14)

8. If you abide in Me, and My words abide in you, you will ask what you desire, and it shall be done for you. (John 15:7)

My words abide in you? Obedience to the commandments of Christ is the only way.

If you are not an obedient believer

"If anyone does not abide in Me, he is cast out as a branch and is withered; and they gather them and throw them into the fire, and they are burned." (John 15:6)

Notes;

Anyone who breaks the community with Christ turns out to be useless, and one has already destroyed himself. It is here aimed at the final judgment, but it is so certain that it is as if it has already taken place.

-The Christian who does not stay with Christ suffers the same fate as the barren branch.

"Now we know that God does not hear sinners; but if anyone is a worshiper of God and **does His will**, He hears him." (John 9:31)

74

9. Can a double-minded person expect to receive any-thing from the Lord? (James 1:5-8)

_____

10. What does the book of James say about being a doer of the word?

(1) James 1:4_____

_____

(2) James 1:22_____

_____

(3) James 2:14_____

_____

(4) James 2:15_____

_____

(5) James 3:13_____

_____

_____

11. As a born again believer, we receive all things from the Lord with an open and willing heart. Is it the same in your life? (Philippians 2:14)

_____

_____

12. What does James 4:7 mean?

_____

_____

13. What is needed for prayer answers? (1 Timothy 2:8)

_____

_____

14. If...

Let us read Matthew 7:13.

"Enter by the **narrow** gate; for wide is the gate and broad is the way that leads to destruction, and there are many who go in by it."

To get through the narrow gate, one has to strip off a lot. (The actions of the flesh)

76

Everything that has to do with greed, an unforgiving spirit, self-ishness, and self-righteousness, must be undressed.
-You have to deny yourself.

Example;
If you do not believe the mission commandment from the Lord, you have not bowed down into the narrow gate and started to walk the narrow path. Instead, you have entered the wide gate that leads to the broad road of compromise and disobedience.

Sad to say, verse 14 shows us that there are not many believers that will humble themselves and obey the Lord.

Do you remember?
Those who do not bear fruit, like the branch of the tree. You will be cut off and thrown into the fire.

Notes;
To follow the Lord the way He says is not at all difficult. Humbleness to the Savior is the key to enter into His Lordship.
-Pride brings unwillingness. Unwillingness never brings anything else than fleshly satisfaction.

Notes;

_____

_____

_____

Answers to Lesson 8
Obedience brings Revelations and Prayer answers

3. "For the Son of Man has come to seek and to save that which was lost." (Luke 19:10)

4. They shall be preached to by all those who believe.

In your daily life, you shall be a witness for Christ to those who live in darkness.

9. No.

Double-minded; vacillating: to waver in mind, will, or feeling: hesitate in choice of opinions or courses.

10.
(1) Patience must lead to action.

(2) Hearing the word must lead to action.

There is an alarming statement at the end of this verse; "But be doers of the word, and not hearers only, deceiving yourselves." (James 1:22)

Deceiving yourself; Misreckon.
Definition of misreckon; To reckon (what God's word says) wrongly.

Countless 'believers' that I have met deny the mission com-
mandment in Mark 16:15, and nevertheless exclaiming 'we see.'
Then there is no question if they live in the truth or not. They are
deceived. (Hebrews 13:9)
-Sad to say, most of them belong to a so-called 'church.'
(Remember question 2? Stand thine own)

(3) Faith must lead to the deed.

(4) Compassion must lead to deeds.

(5) Wisdom must make itself known in action.

11. ?

Let's read Philippians 2:14.
"Do all things without complaining and disputing."

We read the word disputings; Greek: dialogismos. It means; De-
bate-dispute-doubtful.

let us read Luke 9:46 from King James version;
"Then there arose a reasoning among them, which of them
should be greatest."

In this verse, we see that reasoning arose among them. The reasoning is dialogismos from Greek.
-Let us take a look at what that is.

First, we read the last part in 2 Corinthians 10:5; "Bringing every thought into captivity to the obedience of Christ."
-This is how we should deal with ever thought coming to us throughout the day. And this can only be done through spiritual discernment.

Ok, back to Luke 9:46.
When a thought is coming, we must capture it. (By not entertaining it)
But the disciples in this passage did not do that. They believed (agreed) the thought (reasoning), and this dialogissmos thought brings with him a demon of confusion.
-And then argue, debate, dispute, and the misunderstanding of God's word is at hand.

Now you know why Philippians 2:14 states it very clear when it becomes our attitude/willingness towards God's word.

12. James 4:7 - Submit yourself. Means: be under obedience - obey. (God)

13. Holiness is necessary for prayer answers.

80

Notes;

Blind by own choice

The entire earth community is just ahead of judgment, turning to sports, fun, drinking, and festivals.

This was the case before the fall of Rome, Nineveh, Tire, Sodom, Jerusalem, and Babylon. Everyone danced and drank their last judgment hours.

-They are all deceived by a sense of security.

The same is true in most so-called congregations. They dance to sing their praises to end with mighty amen. On the outside of their doors, Satan works feverishly with great success in tricking people into the path who leads to eternal damnation. They couldn't care less.

-Their sense of security also deceives them.

Notes;

_____

_____

_____

Full steam ahead

Until we all are dead
said the one
who feels safe and secured
in his playground

Judgment is coming
the lost keep running
after whats safe and stunning

Believers hide themselves
far away from Christ himself
that will not end well

Why don't we wanna obey
when Christ warns us
about that horrible judgment day

Instead, we sing and dance
shouting hallelujah, its like a romance

Repent right now
and lay your fleshly life down
to Him who has the eternal crown

Sin's supreme demand for acceptance

Judgment? So what! We should all die once, they say, as they dance further down the street into the intoxication of sin. Prosperous carefree nations have fun on their way to the end.

The text on the gravestone God will place on our society is the same He put on Noah's; "**And did not know until the flood came and took them all…**" (Matthew 24:39)

'Believers' sit in their permanent places Sunday after Sunday

-After three or four standard songs of praise is over, a pastor emerges, who is not at all interested in the lost sheep of the Lord on the outside of 'his' barley.
-The vast majority of them have the same kind of 'sense of security' as the unsaved, even though they may not attend the same type of festivities as they do, they say; What I do is good and good enough - Don't tell me otherwise!

A believer who does not seek those who are on the path of perdition with the Lord's life-saving gospel is lost himself.

Bad fruit

Scripture is something not to be taken for granted. It will cost you to get into an understanding of it. If the unwillingness is advancing in your life, we see here in simplicity the fruits of the flesh take on your life.

The Lord says in Ephesians 5:17; Wherefore be ye not **unwise**, but understanding what the will of the Lord is.

The word **unwise** means; Stupid - ignorant - fool(ish) - unbelieving - unwise - **Egoistic**.

**Millions of 'believers' on planet earth are ignorant of the
preaching the Gospel of Jesus Christ to the lost.**

1. What is sin? (1 John 3:4)

_____

_____

The dominion of sin applies to all

Our sin and sin nature, which is traced back to the first fall of
sin, when sin entered the world. Because of Adam's sin, all men
have come under God's judgment; It is shown by death, which is
the punishment of sin has penetrated to all. (Romans 5:12)
But not only the guilt of sin but also the nature of sin has entered
the human race. Just as all people are sinners, so too is all man
tainted by sin. Sin has invaded even human nature so that it has
become sinful and corrupt.
(Romans 8:5, Romans 8:3, Romans 7:23)

The flesh is not obedient to God's law, nor can it be, because the
desire of the flesh is enmity to God. (Romans 8:7)
Sin is, in its very essence, hatred of God, and this animosity of
God is the source from which evil deeds flow from.

Sin is almost a personified being, which has dwelt in the center
of the personality, and which causes man to do evil, though ac-

cording to his inner man, says yes to the law of God.
(Romans 7:17)

But what was impossible for man by his power (Romans 7:18),
and impossible for the law, made God possible by sending his
Son. (Romans 8:3)

2. Unbelief.

What is unbelief?
Unbelief is the opposite of faith, negative attitude of man to-
wards God. It is a denial of what faith holds in connection with
God and his world.
Furthermore, it is disobedience to God, unwillingness, and op-
position to Him.

(1) Those who do not believe in God. Those who deny the Lord;
Unbeliever.

(2) Those who proclaim to believe, those who say Jesus is their
Lord but is not willing to do what He says, is also an unbeliever.

Listen;
"Do not be unequally yoked together with unbelievers. For what
fellowship has righteousness with lawlessness? And what communion has light with darkness?" (2 Corinthians 6:14)

Unbelievers; Greek; Apistos; One who does not believe. Infidel.

Do you remember what infidel means?

Infidel is a derogatory term used when someone does not believe the central principles of one's faith.

-Unbelievers in this context mean in all simplicity; Disobedience to God.

3. Examples of unbelievers;

(1) **Luke 12:43-46**

"Blessed is that servant whom his master will find so doing when he comes. Truly, I say to you that he will make him ruler over all that he has. But if that servant says in his heart, 'My master is delaying his coming,' and begins to beat the male and female servants, and to eat and drink and be drunk, the master of that servant will come on a day when he is not looking for him, and at an hour when he is not aware, and will cut him in two and appoint him his portion with the **unbelievers**."

(2) **1 Corinthians 6:6**

"But brother goes to law against brother, and that before unbelievers!"

(3) **2 Corinthians 4:4**

"Whose minds the god of this age has blinded, who do not believe, lest the light of the gospel of the glory of Christ, who is the image of God, should shine on them."

4. Unbelieving;

(1) Titus 1:15
"To the pure, all things are pure, but to those who are defiled and unbelieving, nothing is pure, but even their mind and conscience are defiled."

(2) Revelation 21:8
"But the cowardly, **unbelieving**, abominable, murderers, sexually immoral, sorcerers, idolaters, and all liars shall have their part in the lake which burns with fire and brimstone, which is the second death."

Notes;

_____

_____

_____

_____

_____

_____

_____

5. Infidel;

(1) 1 Timothy 5:8 KJV

"But if any provide not for his own, and specially for those of his own house, he hath denied the faith, and is worse than an **infidel**."

(2) **2 Corinthians 6:15**

"And what accord has Christ with Belial? Or what part has a believer with an **unbeliever?**"

Two who claims to believe come together. One of them is living a life in obedience in Mark 16:15, and the others do not believe that Mark 16:15 is his call. Can this be a fellowship or not?

_____

_____

6. So far, in this book, you have heard many things from the Lord. What does Hebrews 3:7-9 means?

_____

_____

_____

7. What does the hardening of your heart do to your divine understanding? (Ephesians 4:18)

_____

_____

_____

8. They were spoken to by the prophets, but they did not understand (did not hear) why? (Zechariah 7:12)

_____

_____

9. What will happen to the unbeliever in Hebrews 3:12-16?

_____

_____

10. What does Hebrews 4:5-7 tells us about the result of disobedience?

_____

_____

11. Is this you? (Psalm 17:10)

"They are enclosed in their own prosperity and have shut up their hearts to pity; with their mouths, they make exorbitant claims and proudly and arrogantly speak." (Psalm 17:10 - AMPC)

Your answer;_____

_____

Notes;

_____

_____

_____

_____

_____

_____

_____

_____

Answers to Lesson 9
Blind by own choice

1. Sin is an offense.

Lets read 1 John 3:4; "Whoever commits sin also commits law-lessness, and sin is lawlessness."

Sin is an offense; Disobedience to God's will and transgressions of his law. But sin is also unbelieving (disobedient): violation of his person and mockery of his character.
It is an element of selfishness in every sin, but what is directed against God is a more important aspect of sin than that which glorifies the self. Sin is no less of goodness or lack of goodness. Sin is something active, evil, and destructive.

The strongest Hebrew word for sin is; Pesha. Pesha stands for turning against God in open rebellion.
Sin is not only defiant disobedience to the law but disbelief and rejection of the gospel. (John 16:9 - Romans 10:16)

5.
(2). No, it cannot and shall not be anything between the two of them.

The one who does not believe the great commission in Mark 16:15 is living in darkness.
The obedient one is living in the light. (2 Corinthians 6:14)

6. If you hear His voice today, do not harden your heart.

7. Because of ignorance to the Lord and His word, they are darkened in their understanding.

8. They made their hearts like flint so they could not hear.

Can you see what will happen if you are hardening your heart against God's commandment to you?

Your answer;_____

_____

_____

9. A <u>disobedient</u> heart makes you fall away from the living God.

"<u>Beware, brethren</u>, **lest there be in any of you an evil heart of unbelief in departing from the living God**; but exhort one another daily, while it is called "Today," lest any of you be hardened through the deceitfulness of sin. For we have become partakers of Christ if we hold the beginning of our confidence steadfast to the end, while it is said; "Today, if you will hear His voice, do not harden your hearts as in the rebellion." (Hebrews 3:12-16)

10. They shall not enter the Lord's Rest.

Reveal Satan or obey him

1. Thoughts

'Thought' in Scripture is often closely related to the heart as an expression of the innermost of man, of the whole personality. One consequence of the fall was that the thoughts and inventions of the human heart became evil. (Genesis 6:5)

The spiritual warfare

Because a Christian is in a battle between the flesh and the Spirit, (Romans 8:12), he needs spiritual weapons to overthrow ungodly thought structures and capture every thought under obedience to Christ.

"For though we walk in the flesh, we do **not war** according to the flesh. For the weapons of our warfare are not carnal but mighty in God for pulling down strongholds, casting down arguments and every high thing that exalts itself against the knowledge of God, **bringing every thought into captivity to the obedience of Christ**." (2 Corinthians 10:3-5)

In this scripture, we read the word **war**. The first thing you must think about is; It does not only say that you are in a war. It says we do not war according to the flesh. Here we see that it is not a matter if you are having a troubled time or not: it shows you that you are in a constant war. And if you do not know how to fight this war, it is because the flesh is controlling your life.

Therefore there is no other option than by usage of your free will and boldness to enter the arena and fight Satan with revelations from the written word of God.

Discernment you need every second of your life.
Not only shall we discern the words that are spoken to us by other humans, but we shall discern every spirit that talks to us, shows us things, telling us what to do in all aspects throughout your day.

2. Why do we need to discern everything in all matters? (1 Peter 5:8)

_____

_____

_____

3. What will happen if you are not functioning in the spiritual discernment? (Romans 12:2)

_____

_____

_____

_____

4. What did Jesus do with the disciples in Mark 16:14?

_____

_____

_____

5. Are you a disciple? (John 10:27)

Your answer;_____

6. What is God the Father (Yahweh) telling you to do regarding His Son Jesus? (Matthew 17:5)

_____

_____

7. What are you if you know the commandments of God but do not want to obey them? (1 John 2:4-5)

_____

96

_____

8. Jesus asks you this; Is your door open to let Me be 100% Lord in your life? (Revelation 3:17)

Your answer;_____

_____

_____

_____

Notes;

_____

_____

_____

_____

_____

_____

Answers to Lesson 10
Reveal Satan or obey him

2. Because Satan walks about like a roaring lion, seeking whom he may devour. (1 Peter 5:8)

3. Answer; You will live in total deception.

"And do not be conformed to this world, but be transformed by the renewing of your mind, that you may **prove** (discern) what is that good and acceptable and perfect will of God."
(Romans 12:2)

4. He rebuked them for their unbelief and hardness of heart.

Here we see that if you do not believe the Mission commandment in Mark 16:15, you are hardening your heart.

6. Listen to Him - Do what He says.

7. If you know the truth but don't do it, you are a liar.

98

Notes;

_____

_____

_____

_____

_____

_____

_____

_____

_____

_____

_____

_____

Are you seeking the Lord?

1. There is an alarming statement in Matthew 7:22-23, where Jesus speaks to those who did not have a close relationship with him.

What does verse 22-23 say?

_____

_____

_____

2. How to start seeking the Lord? (1 Peter 2:2)

_____

_____

_____

_____

3. The Gold and the mine

A gold digger's faith and action drive him out into the field to look for this precious metal.

(1) What do we need to dig for Gold?

We need to set aside time, plan where to go, and get the right gear. When this is done, we determined to go to the area were to execute our plan.

(2) What do we need to act on Mark 16:15?

Believe the mission commandment. Then you must act on what you believe. When we act like the Gold digger, we learn day by day how to extract Gold that is hidden in the ground.

When you walk in faith, when you are determined in your actions on God's word, you will learn how to reach the lost. One step at a time in faith brings wisdom and understanding for you to give to the unsaved.

4. Ask, seek, look, knock, never give up.

Can you mention six things in Matthew 7:7-8, that refers to the doer of the word, and not the unwilling listener? (James 1:22)

(1)_____ (2)_____

(3)_____ (4)_____

(5)_____ (6)_____

5.

You and Him

If you shall seek the Lord
you and him
needs to be in one accord

If not
you will be stranded ashore

To give your heart to the Lord
is not to walk after this worlds accord

Lay down your life
seek the author of life

With all your heart
you will be able
to find the Father's heart

Those who take this light
will end up in heavy Fahrenheit

This is how serious this is
get off this worlds bliss

6. What does 2 Corinthians 11:4 say about your faith?

_____

_____

7. Exercise - closing the gates of the senses - resting the flesh.

In Matthew 6:6, we see how to seek the Lord quietly. Sounds, tastes, smells, hearing, emotions, and most important, namely, capturing the mind of Satan.
-If we do not practice this in our everyday lives, we will not grow into the spirituality this scripture shows us.

"But you, when you pray, go into your room, and when you have shut your door, pray to your Father who is in the secret place; and your Father who sees in secret will reward you openly." (Matthew 6:6)

Close your door to this world. Use your spiritual eyes to seek the Lord inward into the world of the Holy Spirit.

Notes;

_____

_____

_____

Answers to Lesson 11
Are you seeking the Lord?

1. I never knew you.

"Many will say to Me in that day, 'Lord, Lord, have we not prophesied in Your name, cast out demons in Your name, and done many wonders in Your name?' And then I will declare to them, '**I never knew you; depart from Me**, you who practice lawlessness!" (Matthew 7:22-23)

These people Jesus are talking to here, are people who have been ministering. They have healed and delivered in the name of the Lord.
-Still, Jesus rejects them.

One who does not seek God as he should, will not discern spiritually as he should.
-Spiritual discernment is the torch of a Christian's life in a world in which everything lies in the evilness.

If you do not seek God as you should, you will not have any relationship with Him either. It is only through obedience to Christ that we come into the understanding of spiritual realities.

Notes;

_____

_____

2. Seek the pure milk of God's word.

"As newborn babes, desire the (1) pure milk of the word, (2) that you may grow thereby." (1 Peter 2:2)

(1) It is the Lord through His word that we shall start to seek the same day as we become born again.

(2) At the end of this verse, you see that to seek the Lord through His word is the right way to grow in Him.

When we seek the Lord wholeheartedly, you will start to draw nearer and nearer to him. His personality and character is the greatest achievement for us to get a hold of in our lives.

4.

"**Ask**, and it will be given to you; **seek**, and you will find; **knock**, and it will be opened to you. For everyone who **asks** receives, and he who **seeks** finds, and to him who **knocks** it will be opened." (Matthew 7:7-8)

The verbs 'Ask',' Seek' and 'knock' express in their grammatical form something persistent. We shall continue, we will keep on asking, searching, and knocking.

(1) **Ask, and it will be given to you.**

What are you asking the Lord about?

_____

_____

_____

_____

Most believers ask, but it is for their selfish lifestyle. Very few ask about revelations regarding God's will.

(2) Seek, and you will find.

The seeking is the conscious effort to get through the natural means to God himself - set our minds continuously toward God in all our experiences, to direct our minds and hearts toward him through the means of His revelation.

(3) Knock, and it will be opened for you.

Knocking is an attitude of never giving up. (Perseverance)
It is the Lord's door we knock on, and it is His presence and revelations (secrets from heaven) that is of importance.

Obedience is the only key
Seek His presence.
Seek His wisdom.
Seek His revelations.

Seek His will by acting on His word.

-This is way more than to pray with a long list in your hands of what you need.

6. Believers must not be seduced.

2 Corinthians 10:5 shows us how to deal with spoken untruth against us.

Notes;

_____

_____

_____

_____

_____

_____

_____

_____

Idolatry - An abomination to the Lord

Idolatry connotes the worship of something or someone other than God as if it were God.

Synonyms for idolatry;
Extreme admiration, love, worship, adoring, glorification, or reverence for something or someone, or a person -'church' in place of God.

Christ never temp or seduce anyone
That means; He will never mislead you or tell you it is ok to walk the wrong way when it becomes to churches or fellowship. What Christ demands of you is that you repent, become born again, and start to follow him. Then Christ will be your Lord. If you are not filled with His word, Jesus cannot teach you much.

John 14:26 shows us that when you wholeheartedly follow Christ through His word, The Holy Ghost will teach you all things. If you are acting on what is written here, you will not go the wrong way. Your feelings and other people around you may tell you otherwise, but it is Christ who is our Lord, not our feelings.

Satan is the one that seduces

Satan wants you to go to churches and congregations that seem to be right but are false. Satan loves that you do not take the word of God seriously, but follow your feelings and intuitions instead.

I cannot urge enough the importance of staying close to the Lord at the time we are living now. But if you do not take Christ seriously, you will not be able to see the truth as you should.

1. What is written in 1 Peter 4:11?

_____

_____

_____

2. What does Proverbs 29:18 say about divine revelations?

_____

_____

_____

_____

3. Idolatry - Worshipping idols is forbidden. God says no, the man says Yes.

(1) Can a man lie?

Your answer;_____

(2) Can God lie? (Titus 1:2)

Your answer;_____

4. What does the Lord say in Acts 7:48?

_____

_____

5. What does the Bible say about idolatry?
(Romans 1:23)

_____

6. What does idolatry consist in? (Exodus 20:4-5)

_____

7. Do idolators worship images? (Isaiah 44:16-18)

_____

8. Is idolatry incompatible with the service of God?
(1 Samuel 7:3-4)

_____

9. Are idolators looking to other gods? (Hosea 3:1)

_____

10. Do idolators worship the true God by an image?
(Psalm 106:19-21)

_____

11. How many ways are there to the Father in heaven?
(John 14:6)

_____

Notes;

_____

_____

_____

_____

Answers to Lesson 12
Idolatry - An abomination to the Lord

1. If you do not enter into a position with your life so you can receive personal revelations from the Lord, you will be deceived.

2. Without Divine Revelations, people will perish.

"Where there is no **vision**, the people **perish**: but he that keepeth the law, happy is he." (Proverbs 29:18 KJV)

We read the word **vision**, Hebrew; Chazown. It means; **Revelations**.

The next word in Proverbs 29:18 is **perish**, Hebrew; Para, and it means; **Spiritual death - backslide**.

If you backslide into spiritual death, there is no way that you can teach the truth, no matter how big 'your church' is.

Remember this verse?
"Jesus said to him, "I am the way, the truth, and the **life**. No one comes to the Father except through Me." (John 14:6)

If you have Jesus Christ as Lord, you have life. But if you have backslid into spiritual death, you are nothing but dead. Then Jesus Christ cannot be your Lord.

3.
Can a man lie? Yes.

Can God lie? No.

4. I do not live in a house made by hands.

Again we see that it is the people who have surrendered their lives to the Lord and do what He says who is the only church.

5. It is changing the glory of God into an image.

6. Bowing down to images. (Following-Trusting)

7. Yes.

8. Yes.

9. Yes.

The raisin cakes mentioned in Hosea 3:1 were used in the Ba'al worship.

10. Yes.

11. One way.

Idolatry - Part 2

1. Would God send a man to earth that is higher than a man to gather His people, without writing about it in the Bible? (John 3:16-18)

_____

2. Is Virgin Mary a co-mediator between God and humanity? (1 Timothy 2:5)

_____

3. **When you voice out Hail Mary mother of God, you are praying into the spiritual realm.**

What does the second commandment say about this? (Exodus 20:4-6)

v4 _____

_____

114

_____

v5_____

_____

_____

v6_____

_____

_____

4. What is idolatry described as?

(1) Galatians 5:19-20_____

_____

(2) Deuteronomy 16:22_____

_____

(3) Psalm 115:4-8_____

_____

_____

5. What do those who idolize do?

(1) Deuteronomy 8:19 - Jeremiah 18:15_____

_____

(2) Ezekiel 44:10_____

_____

(3) Ezekiel 20:39_____

_____

(4) 2 Kings 22:17 - Jeremiah 16:11_____

_____

(5) 2 Chronicles 19:2-3_____

_____

(6) Isaiah 65:3_____

_____

(7) Romans 1:21-23_____

_____

116

(8) Psalm 97:7_____

_____

(9) Hosea 4:12_____

_____

(10) Isaiah 45:20_____

_____

6. What does Revelation 21:8 say about what will happen to all the idolators?

_____

_____

7. Can you now see why the wrath of God will fall on those who practice idolatry? (Exodus 20:4-5)

_____

_____

_____

8. Why did Jesus speak the parable of the yeast to his disciples? (Matthew 16:5-12)

_____

_____

_____

_____

_____

It is only when you walk the way the Lord wants you will know the truth.

"And you shall know the truth, and the truth shall make you free." (John 8:32)

Notes;

_____

_____

_____

_____

_____

Answers to Lesson 13
Idolatry - Part 2

1. No, He would not. God sent His only begotten Son to save the world - No one else!

2. No. Jesus Christ is.

"For there is one God and one Mediator between God and men, the Man Christ Jesus." (1 Timothy 2:5)

3. (v4) You shall not make for yourself a carved image - any likeness of anything that is in heaven above, or that is in the earth beneath, or that is in the water under the earth.

(v5) You shall not bow down to them nor serve them. For I, the Lord your God, am a jealous God, visiting the iniquity of the fathers upon the children to the third and fourth generations of those who hate Me.

If you do worship Virgin Mary or any other dead saints, you bring the wrath of God into your life and generations after you. The only way out of this is to repent to Christ, be born again, and follow him the way He wants.

(v6) But showing mercy to thousands, to those who love Me and keep My commandments.

Throughout the scripture, we see that to do what God says is the only way to His grace and mercy.

4.

(1) It is a work of the flesh.

(2) Hateful to God.

(3) Vain and foolish.

5.

(1) Forget God.

(2) Go astray from God.

(3) Pollute the name of God.

(4) Idolators forsake God.

(5) Hate God.

(6) Provoke God.

(7) Are vain in their imagination, ignorant and foolish.

(8) Idolators boast of their idolatry.

(9) Ask counsel of their gods.

(10) Look to idols for deliverance.

6. They will all end in the lake of fire.

If the one who is idolizing will stop doing it, repent and turn to Christ with his whole heart, he will be forgiven.

-Repent means stop doing. (Never again)

7. ?

8. This is what Jesus says when something is almost true; Is it a little lie (leaven) in one's learning: **it's all a lie**. (The whole dough is permeated)

Leaven is fermented dough, which in particular was stored in water in older times to be used later as a fermenter in a freshly prepared dough. In the scriptures, leaven is used as a picture of impurity, evil, and lies, which in this age tend to penetrate everything.

Notes;

_____

_____

_____

_____

_____

Epilogue

It is only when Christians obey the mission command in Mark 16:15 that life begins to live to the fullest.

A heart that knocks after continuing what Jesus came to earth to give his life for, a heart that pounders for the unsaved to hear the fantastic gospel of Jesus Christ.

The centerpiece in a Christian's life is preaching the gospel of Jesus Christ. When believers do not want this, they have failed at what Christianity is.

If you are not willing, nor do you think you are going to be a witness wherever you are in the world, you have to ask yourself if you were born again at all.

It is not possible to be filled with the Holy Spirit, live in a life of revelations, and would not obey the Lord's commands.

One may have been reborn once, but if we do not begin one's life in obedience, and end up in a so-called church, one will die spiritually. More information can be found in Hebrews 5.

Believers do not seek God. Most of them go to a place where a pastor says; This is God's house - The Lord has put me here to be your pastor. Here you will have your spiritual food, give ten percent of your income, and holy gifts.

-This type of church has taken the place of Christ. If you are part of such an assembly, there are no other words to say; The Lord says Go out into the world. Then you shall have nothing to do with the unbelievers. (Disobedient)

Either you live in victory with the Lord, or you sit in the benches to justify yourself.

-It's time to take Christ seriously!

Notes;

_____

_____

_____

_____

_____

_____

_____

Mark 16:15

Why don't you want to go
when Satan shouts ho ho

He binds and blinds
torture and kill
all believers do
is to lay in their hammock
and say, this is my will

Jesus Christ wants to gather His lost sheep
stop listening to Uriah Heep

The lost cannot be found
if you also are lost
traveling fast southbound

124

Notes;

Thank you very much
for reading this book

I hope it has been an inspiration to you, and that you will take
the plunge into the power ministry our Lord and Savior Jesus
Christ has for you.

It is essential to get into a Biblical understanding of who our
God is. Lay down your life, surrender everything to the Lord our
God. He said that signs and wonders would follow those who
believe.

All the old, all of the carnal desires, everything that goes against
the Lord's written Word, must be repented from in your life. All
knowledge that you need must come from the Lord. He will give
to all who are willing to lay down their lives and obey His
commandments.

Take it, seek the Lord with all your heart, with all your strength,
with all your mind.
Then you will have it.

Stay updated

There are new books on its way. Stay tuned to our website for new releases.

www.SecretRevelations.com

May the Lord bless you and yours abundantly.

Rune Larsen

Pain or any sickness, be healed in Jesus name!

www.ingramcontent.com/pod-product-compliance
Lightning Source LLC
LaVergne TN
LVHW021346080426

835508LV00020B/2135